Brutalia

By Zupagrafika
David Navarro & Martyna Sobecka

-

Foreword: Alessandro Benetti

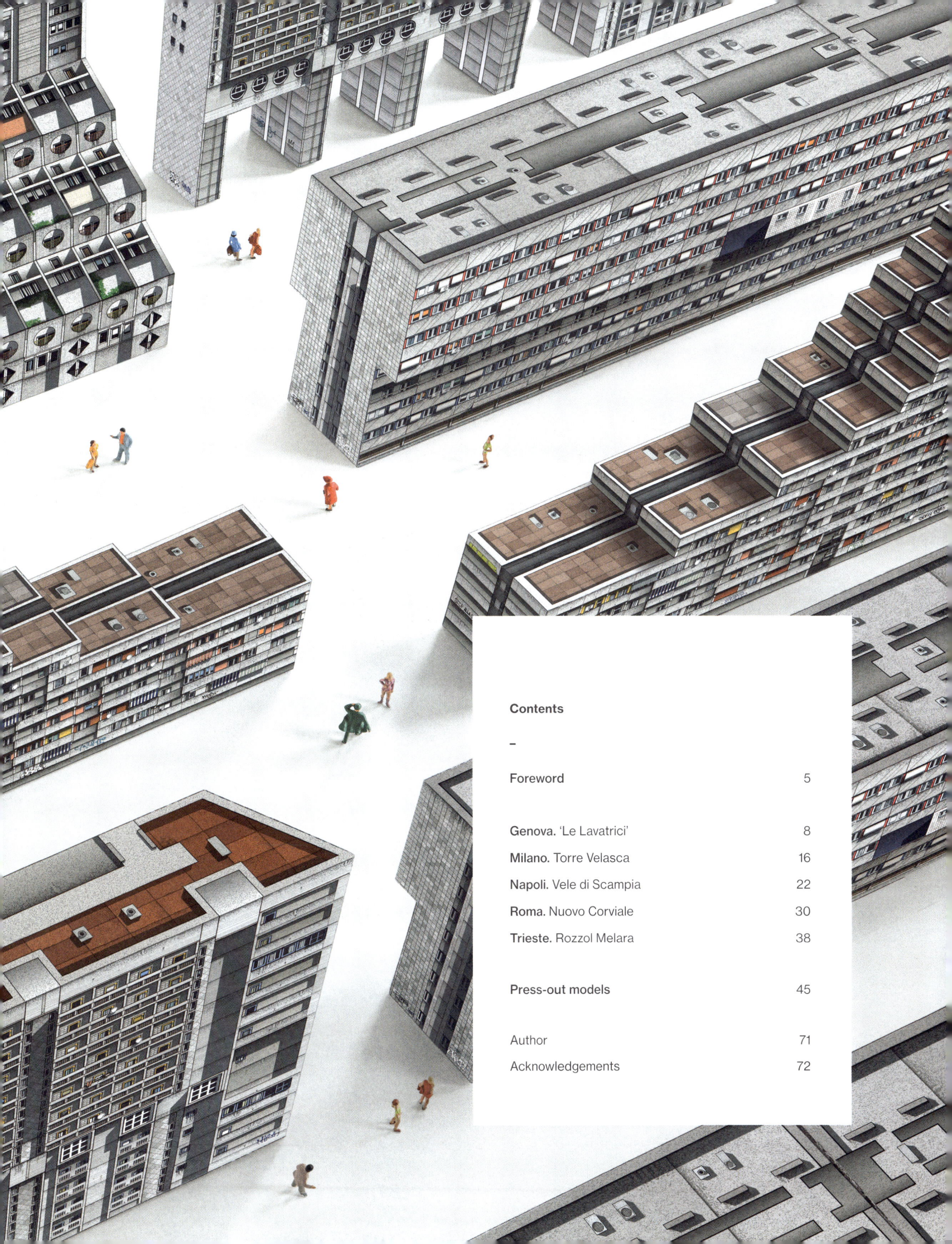

Contents

—

Foreword   5

Genova. 'Le Lavatrici'   8
Milano. Torre Velasca   16
Napoli. Vele di Scampia   22
Roma. Nuovo Corviale   30
Trieste. Rozzol Melara   38

Press-out models   45

Author   71
Acknowledgements   72

Concrete Geographies:
Italian Brutalism and the Search for a New Scale

Milan's Torre Velasca, completed in 1958 on the ashes of a section of the city that was devastated by WWII, is an ambiguous and iridescent object that escapes the style-based taxonomies of historical–critical narratives about architecture. Designed by a trio of leading figures of Italian Rationalism – Lodovico Barbiano di Belgiojoso, Enrico Peressutti and Ernesto Nathan Rogers, partners of the BBPR firm – it also served as the Trojan horse that helped the national delegation to the 11th International Congresses of Modern Architecture (CIAM) in Otterlo in 1959 to destabilise from within the very principles of the Modern Movement. The building is classified in official histories as one of the highest expressions of *neoliberty*, according to Reyner Banham's scathing definition of it in *The Architectural Review*. The collective imagination, however, intuitively associates it with brutalism. It is impossible, and perhaps unhelpful, to unravel the knots of this decades-old *querelle* in the brief space of this introduction. Rather, it is of interest here to acknowledge the crucial role of the most talked-about of the Milanese high-rises of the second half of the twentieth century in propelling Italian architecture beyond the modern paradigms that informed it in the previous three decades. The construction of the Velasca opened a new epoch, in many ways brutal on a conceptual level – for the disproportion of the mass scale and for the violence of the debate around the discipline, its tasks and its objects – and very often brutalist in its style.

The history of Italian brutalism, understood as a local reinterpretation of that unpolished, all-concrete sensibility that emerged in parallel in England and France in the early 1950s, is full of exquisite works: precious inserts in the delicate historic centres of the peninsula; daring attempts at ethical–aesthetic revolution in the standardised bourgeois province; innovative proposals for *loisir* architecture, private or public, in the city, at the seaside or in the mountains; disturbing and sublime pre- and post-conciliar churches; places of production and infrastructures in a country trying to expand despite crises. There is, however, a corpus of works that are identified in the first place with the season of the Brutalist *Bel Paese*: these are the large housing complexes that sprang up on the fringes of major cities, starting in the mid-1960s and continuing until the early 1980s, on a long wave of endless delays and economic difficulties.

Amphitheatre on the western side of Nuovo
Corviale housing estate in Rome

Their story has a precise year zero. In 1962, Law 167, born out of the remnants of the more ambitious *riforma urbanistica* (urban planning reform) envisioned by Christian Democrat Fiorentino Sullo, assigned top priority to public housing, understood as a pivotal element of planning. Municipalities were given a new, powerful legislative tool for the implementation of the resulting plans: expropriation for reasons of public utility. Amid many contradictions, all brought about by the pressures of landowners and private developers with more or less hidden interests, the most efficient and far-sighted municipal administrations managed to subtract substantial portions of their land from speculation. Rising in these 'protected reserves', on the initiative of the municipalities themselves or of the historic Istituto Autonomo Case Popolari (IACP) founded in 1903, are most of the Italian *grands ensembles* of the 1960s and 1970s, which share many of the joys and sorrows of their French equivalents, on average a decade older.

The city, be it ancient or modern, is almost always a distant backdrop. Unseen geometries 'decorate' the countryside, so colossal as to turn into artificial geographies. Not surprisingly, Vittorio Gregotti's epoch-making essay *L'architettura del territorio* was published in 1966. Gregotti interpreted *territorium* in the Latin meaning of the term, as a 'place of transformation of the earth', an anthropogeographic environment within which architecture is constituted as large-scale semiology – the reference is to the coeval studies of Umberto Eco and Roland Barthes. Gregotti's reflections, along with those on similar themes by Giancarlo De Carlo, Saverio Muratori and Luigi Piccinato, more or less directly inspired a generation of projects that are constructed geographies and describe themselves as such: the Corviale in Rome (Mario Fiorentino and others, 1970–1984) is a peremptory rectilinear dam that carves out the soft undulations of the Roman countryside; the *'Lavatrici'* (The Washing Machines) in Genoa's Pegli 3 neighbourhood (Aldo Luigi Rizzo and Aldo Pino, completed in 1989) clad and geometrise a ridge overlooking the Ligurian Sea; Rozzol Melara in Trieste (Studio Celli-Tognon, 1969–1983) encloses a boundless parade ground in the hills sloping down toward the capital of Friuli; ZEN 2 in Palermo (Vittorio Gregotti and others, 1969–1976) resembles a colossal beehive and invented a previously non-existent morphology in a barren land north of the city.

'The rough, statistical, repetitive, and ultimately truly democratic aesthetic of Corviale and its counterparts transcribes a precise stance against the aesthetic canons of the bourgeois city.'

In all these cases, and in so many coeval and similar ones, the question of scale is closely linked to that of language. Throughout the 1950s, public residential Italy had been built first and foremost through the INA Casa Plan, launched in 1949. In the regime of post-war scarcity, a precise political choice had dictated the use of conventional techniques and materials, managed by low-skilled domestic firms and labour. The intersection between these constraints and the morphological–linguistic studies by architects mainly from Rome – Ludovico Quaroni, Mario Ridolfi – and from

Milan – Franco Albini, Ignazio Gardella – resulted in the production of picturesque urban landscapes, villages of architecture that were modern but far removed from rationalist purism. More than a decade later, in a more technologically advanced context and in the face of the urgency of much larger quantities, a season of experimentation with reinforced concrete and industrial prefabrication also started in Italy.

'Contemporary design culture continues to look for answers for the future of these cumbersome monuments of the twentieth century.'

It was at this time that public housing became brutalist. Abandoning neo-vernacular references, the complexes of the 1960s and 1970s are *architectures au kilomètres* that inherited from Le Corbusier's *cité radieuse* the taste for disproportion and the ambition for self-sufficiency, while interacting with contemporary European research on the exploration of the formal potential of exposed concrete. In this regard, much discussion has focused on the subtle grooves on Corviale's cladding panels. It has been observed that their slight chiaroscuro vibrations do little or nothing to soften the gigantic building mass to which they are applied. This is a sterile criticism, which misunderstands Fiorentino's intentions. The rough, statistical, repetitive, and ultimately truly democratic aesthetic of Corviale and its counterparts transcribes a precise stance against the aesthetic canons of the bourgeois city. It is the recognizable, and quintessentially brutalist, signature of architects often close to communist ideologies, animated by a strong drive for social reform and, in hindsight, obscured by an illusion of demiurgic almightiness.

Time has proven unforgiving to almost all of Italy's brutalist giants, a common fate of countless large-scale residential compounds from the same age all over the Western world and beyond it. In many cases it is difficult to distinguish the responsibilities of planning and architecture from those of (mis)management in turning them into wrecked ghettos of social isolation and crime. Between perhaps improvident demolitions, first that of the infamous '*Vele*' in Scampia (Franz Di Salvo, 1962–1975), and patient attempts at grafting and stitching – exemplary, in this sense, is precisely the case of Corviale – contemporary design culture continues to look for answers for the future of these cumbersome monuments of the twentieth century. Will the recent critical rehabilitation and the newfound popular enthusiasm for their long-disdained brutalist aesthetics help ensure their preservation and transformation into spaces of a pacified, thriving community life? Only the future will tell.

Alessandro Benetti

Architect and PhD candidate in History of Architecture at Université Rennes 2 and Politecnico di Milano, contributor to Domus and editor of Urbano magazine

Pegli 3
Pra' district

Architects: Aldo Luigi Rizzo and Aldo Pino
Built: 1980–1989

8 residential blocks
688 apartments

Genova > 'Le Lavatrici'

Like a gigantic concrete fortress, Aldo Luigi Rizzo and Aldo Pino's 1980s housing complex was built into the cascading hills of the Apennines. Although its official name is Pegli 3, locals refer to it as *'Lavatrici'* (The Washing Machines), due to the rows of prefabricated circular loggia openings along the facades, reminiscent of the Nakagin capsule tower in Tokyo. The construction of this estate was part of Genoa's 1960s suburban plan to provide quick and cheap social housing west of the city. The plan comprised several districts, including the Pra' port district by the Ligurian Sea. This quaint maritime area with its traditional houses, typically not exceeding three floors, was incorporated into the municipality of Genoa in 1926.

Rizzo's design occupies over 50,000 square metres, towering over the old town. The project was completed in 1989, providing housing for over 2,000 residents in almost 700 apartments, scattered along labyrinthine corridors, open air

The open staircases of Pegli 3 have recently been painted in bright colours

The circular openings of the loggias earned the complex the nickname 'The Washing Machines'

◁
The housing complex, port, and neighbouring farmhouses, as seen from Via Scarpanto

△
The centre of Pra' district and the Ligurian Apennines, seen from a loggia opening

staircases, and 'streets in the sky', overlooking the port and the city. Because it includes very little infrastructure or basic facilities like grocery shops and workspaces, *Lavatrici* remains essentially a dormitory to this day, with most dwellers commuting to and from work daily. As is the case for other Italian post-war era housing estates, like Forte Quezzi in Genoa's district of Marassi, in recent years the inevitable debate about the future and the possible demolition of Pegli 3 has surfaced. Some parts of the complex have already undergone refurbishment; in 2019, a painting project started, adding bright colours to some areas of the estate, such as the staircase and balustrades. However, urban planners continue to investigate new ideas in hopes of recovering the functionality and communal spirit *Lavatrici* was intended to cultivate.

Forte Quezzi, also known as *'Biscione'* (The Snake), a residential complex in the Marassi district of Genoa

Central Zone 1
Piazza Velasca

Architects: BBPR
Built: 1958

26 storeys, 106 metres high
Listed in 2011

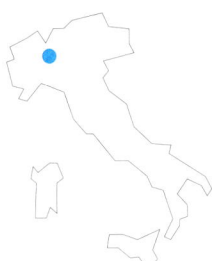

Milano > Torre Velasca

The history of this iconic Milan landmark began in 1932, when four graduates from the Polytechnic of Milan, Gian Luigi Banfi, Lodovico Barbiano di Belgiojoso, Enrico Peressutti and Ernesto Nathan Rogers, started an architectural partnership called BBPR. While their early designs were deeply rooted in rationalism, which flourished in Italy at that time, these young visionary architects were open to the new trends that were slowly gaining ground across Europe and joined the International Congresses of Modern Architecture (CIAM), founded in Switzerland in 1928 by Le Corbusier, Hélène de Mandrot and Sigfried Giedionto. Despite their initial allegiance to Mussolini's government, the four quickly recognised the face of fascism and took a strong opposing stance. Di Belgiojoso and Banfi were imprisoned in the Gusen-Mauthausen Concentration Camp, where Banfi later died, while Ernesto Nathan Rogers went into exile in Switzerland.

It was not until after WWII that the three surviving BBPR founders reunited. Their first new project was a memorial to the victims of Nazi extermination camps in Milan's Monumental Cemetery that paid tribute to the late Banfi and other victims of the holocaust. The three went on to develop social housing projects such as Torri Bianche, erected in Gratosoglio district in the 1960s, and focused on other unique ventures, including furniture, as well as their signature grand design – Torre Velasca.

The distinctive mushroom-shaped tower overlooks the historical centre of Milan

◁
Struts and tie-beams support the protruding residential structure that features approximately 800 apartments

△
The red metal structure has been added recently to support renovation scaffolding

The tower is located in the historical centre of the city, just a few blocks from the famous Milan Cathedral and Sforza Castle. Therefore, the project needed to fit in the historical context despite its modern character. The designers began this task in 1951 and, initially meeting with disapproval from CIAM, decided to combine the regional and the modern, resulting in a structure resembling a mediaeval fortress; it was built in 1958 over ruins left behind by WWII. The 106-metre-, 26-storey-high reinforced concrete construction consists of a narrow tower reserved for offices and shops that supports the protruding residential section, featuring approximately 800 apartments overlooking *centro storico*. The combination of its ambiguous style and peculiar shape earned the building much criticism during its early years. Over time, however, its prestige grew as both Milanesi and architecture aficionados came to appreciate it. Torre Velasca was listed as a historic building in 2011.

△
The 106-metre-high Torre Velasca, designed to resemble a mediaeval fortress, as seen from Piazza Velasca

▷
Torri Bianche is a social housing estate in Gratosoglio neighbourhood, consisting of eight 16-storey tower blocks designed in the early 1960s by the BBPR group

Scampia	Architect: Franz Di Salvo	7 residential blocks
115 hectares	Built: 1962–1975	4 blocks demolished 1997-2020

Napoli > Vele di Scampia

'We are not Gomorrah', proclaims a graffiti sign on the concrete facade of one of the pyramid-shaped blocks on the northern outskirts of Naples. The complex has been making headlines in Italy since the 1980s and in the 2000s, when Roberto Saviono's startling book *Gomorrah* (about the Camorra mafia in Naples) was published, Scampia became well known worldwide. The large sail-like structures, intended to house mainly young families, were designed by Franz Di Salvo, an architect specialised in low-cost post-war social housing. The estate was meant to cultivate collective living, with abundant parks, playgrounds, schools, and other facilities in the vicinity, while apartment size and features were cut to the bone to encourage outdoor life and simultaneously economise the construction. Shared exterior spaces, such as long open corridors, bridges and multi-level suspended staircases connecting the buildings resemble the traditional narrow passages and courtyards of the 'old' vibrant Naples, while simultaneously bringing to mind a dystopian sci-fi city. Bold concrete structures like these were built all over post-war Italy with the intention of remodelling the country's urbanscapes; they served not only for housing estates but also churches, football stadiums and public buildings (Casa del Portuale by Aldo Loris Rossi, erected between 1969 and 1978 for the Naples port offices is one of the most brazen cases in point).

Seven housing blocks in Scampia were designed to resemble large triangular sails

△

The patios feature open staircases and corridors that connect the different building modules

▷

The derelict facades have been covered in street art and graffiti

The seven *Vele* (Sails) were originally intended to house approximately 30,000 people and construction lasted from 1962 until 1975. However, due to a funding shortage, they were never completed. When the devastating Irpinia earthquake left nearly 250,000 people homeless in southern Italy in 1980, the new estate came to be partially occupied by people in need of shelter. Due to the omnipresent chaos the local government faced after the natural disaster, the Scampia population, including many squatters, grew out of control and the social situation deteriorated. The housing complex was soon taken over by organised crime and transformed into a no-go territory for several decades. In an attempt to solve these problems, four of the Sails were demolished, in 1997, 2000, 2003 and 2020. While two more are awaiting imminent demolition, the only remaining building is set to undergo redevelopment.

◁

Only three of the seven original *Vele* buildings are still standing along Antonio Labriola Street

△ ▷

Casa del Portuale, built between 1969 and 1978 in the port of Naples, designed by Aldo Loris Rossi

| Corviale | Architects: Team led by Mario Fiorentino | 3 residential blocks |
| Municipio XII | Built: 1975–1984 | 1,200 apartments |

Roma > Nuovo Corviale

An innovative construction made of reinforced concrete and prefabricated panels was erected in the 1970s and 1980s only 10 km from the ancient landmarks of the Italian capital. When the population of Rome increased by over a million between the 1950s and the 1970s, a quick and efficient response to the resulting housing shortage was needed. The vast suburban areas were considered perfect locations for large blocks of flats ready to accommodate thousands of inhabitants. The architects of the Nuovo Corviale complex, also called *'Il Serpentone'* (The Big Serpent), took the idea of building large to the next level. A team led by Mario Fiorentino designed an entire urbanisation with a single housing unit, nearly one kilometre long, at its core. Stretching up the green hills of the south-western Municipio XII and covering 60 hectares, the estate features 1,200 flats, housing a population of 6,000. It is divided into three main residential structures: a nine-storey double module slab, a parallel three- and four-storey block, connected with suspended pedestrian bridges, and another three- and four-storey building positioned at a 45° angle. Nuovo Corviale was meant to be much more than a sleeping

▷

Nuovo Corviale housing complex features numerous public recreational spaces

▷▷

The main residential building is almost 1 km long and is known as *'Il Serpentone'* (The Big Serpent)

△
Casa Sperimentale and the Sphere guest house, built in the seaside neighbourhood of Fregene, Rome in 1971

▷
The longest Corviale slab is made of two parallel concrete modules connected with passages

district; with facilities like a kindergarten, a school, shops, recreation areas and Roman-like amphitheatres, it could well function as a fully-fledged and almost self-sufficient settlement.

The decline of Corviale began in the 1980s, mainly because its construction was never fully completed and the unfinished fourth floor of the main structure, originally planned to house commerce and services, was used by squatters instead. Throughout years of neglect, the complex was left to deteriorate, and its future became uncertain. However, unlike Casa Sperimentale (another Roman brutalist landmark, built near Fregene beach in 1971 after a design by Giuseppe Perugini, Raynaldo Perugini and Uga De Plaisant), which was left deserted for decades, renovation and social integration plans for Nuovo Corviale are in progress, offering hope that the Serpent will soon see better days.

The debate about the complex's future is ongoing. While some have advocated for its demolition, a redevelopment plan has been approved instead

Rozzol Melara
11 hectares

Architects: Carlo Celli, Luciano Celli, Dario Tognon
Built: 1969–1983

2 L-shaped blocks
648 apartments

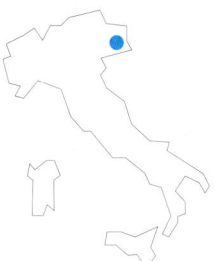

Trieste > Rozzol Melara

In the early 1960s, the *Istituto Autonomo Case Popolari* (Autonomous Council Housing Institute), which is responsible for social housing construction in Italy, found the perfect location for a new settlement, high in the hills west of Trieste, overlooking the city and the Adriatic Sea. The IACP planned an unprecedentedly large residential estate on nearly 11 hectares of land, intended to function as a small, self-sufficient town. Construction work under lead architect Carlo Celli began in 1969 and lasted until 1983, although the first inhabitants were allowed to move in in the late 1970s. The design of the housing project is reminiscent of Le Corbusier's Sainte Marie de La Tourette and features two juxtaposed L-shaped slab blocks, arranged in a large square, resulting in the nickname *'Il Quadrilatero'*. The 15- and 7-storey housing unit sections are supported by concrete pilotis and connected with suspended bridges that form a large cross in the central courtyard and traverse the greenery square between the buildings. In addition to over 600 flats intended to fit 2,500 inhabitants, the complex was to house a civic

The complex is made up of two L-shaped residential units connected by a pedestrian bridge

and health centre, as well as schools, multiple shops, an amphitheatre, and a shared garage. These facilities, along with a custom designed communal green area, realised in collaboration with landscape designer Guido Ferrara, provided the newly formed community with the tools necessary to thrive within this 'machine for living'. However, shortly after construction was completed, problems arose with the management of the complex. In the late 1990s, the estate encountered maintenance and safety issues, and the premises destined for services and communal activities were largely abandoned. The 2002 international contest for young architects, organised by *Azienda Territoriale per l'Edilizia Residenziale* (Territorial Agency for Housing of Trieste), attempted to revive Rozzol Melara; however, no renovation plans for the complex have come to fruition so far.

◁
The two 15- and 7-storey housing blocks accommodate approximately 2,500 people

△
Flats and bridges are accessed through long corridors dotted with circular windows overlooking the estate

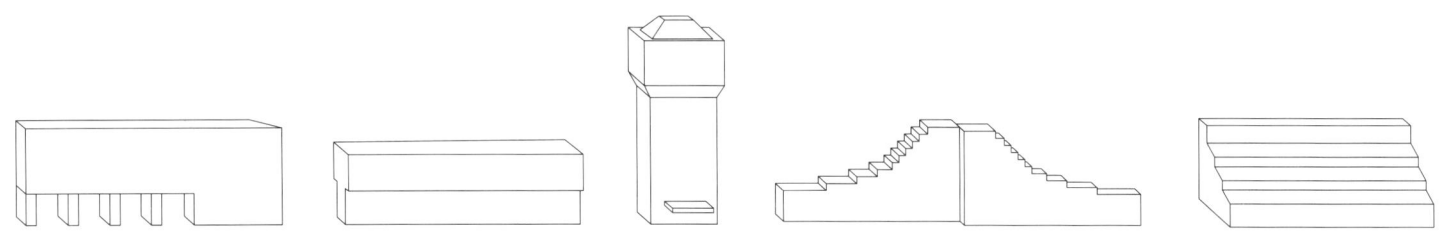

—

Models are die-cut and pre-folded

Carefully press all elements out

Firmly fold all parts before assembling

White glue is recommended

Enjoy!

Genova 'Le Lavatrici'

by Zupagrafika

Genova 'Le Lavatrici'

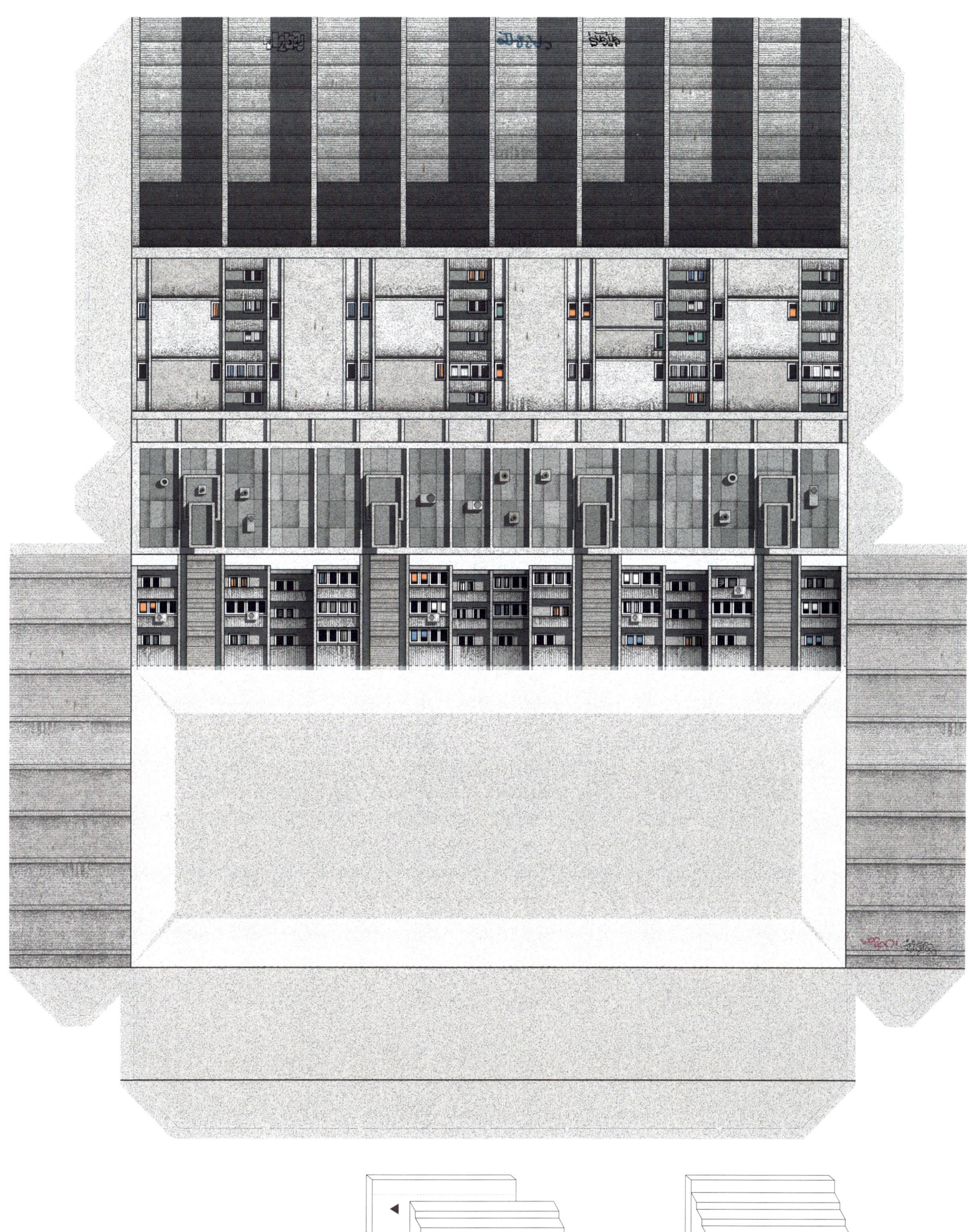

Milano Torre Velasca

A
C
by Zupagrafika

C

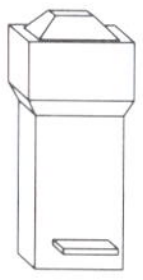

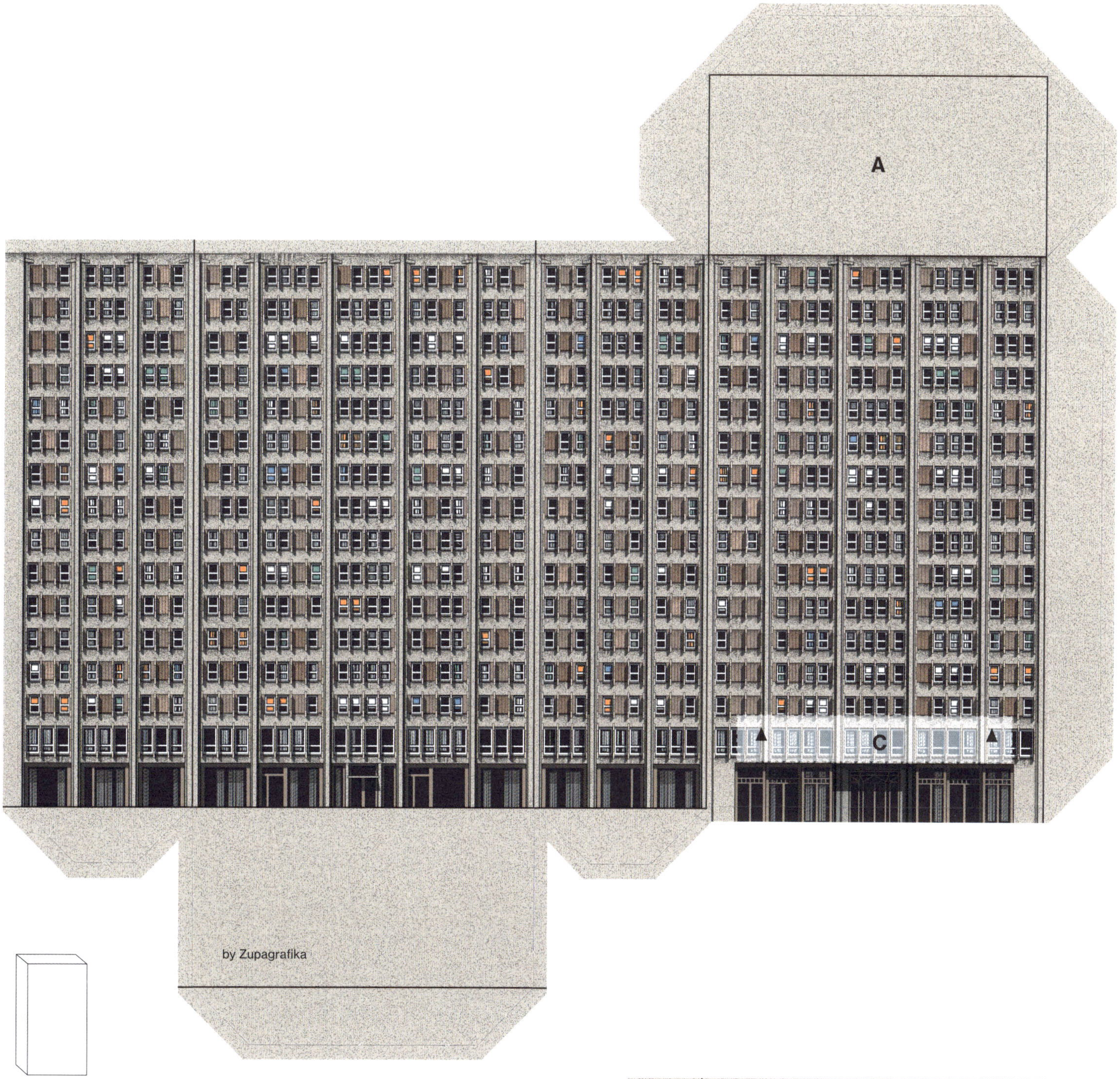

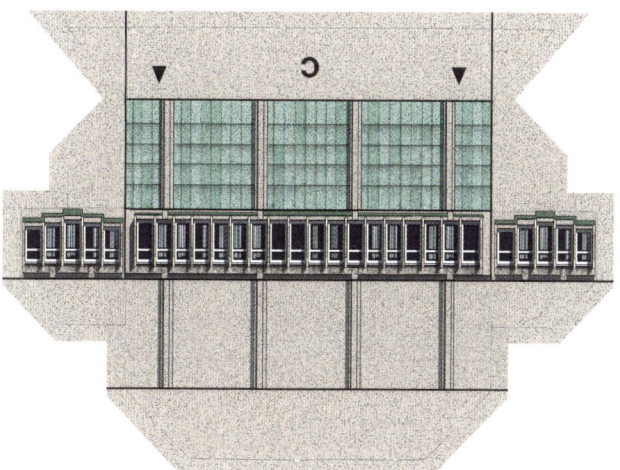

Milano Torre Velasca

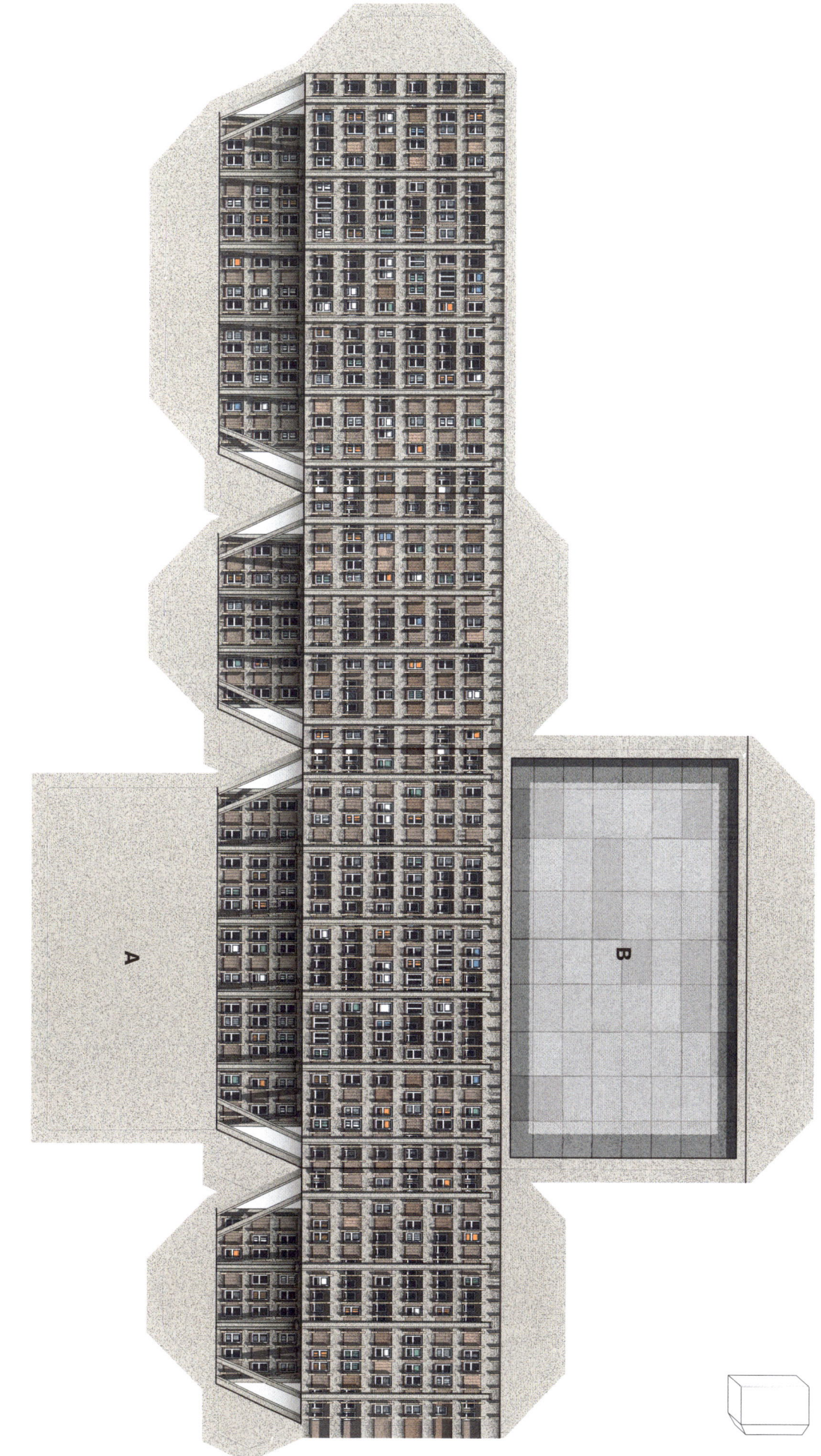

Milano Torre Velasca

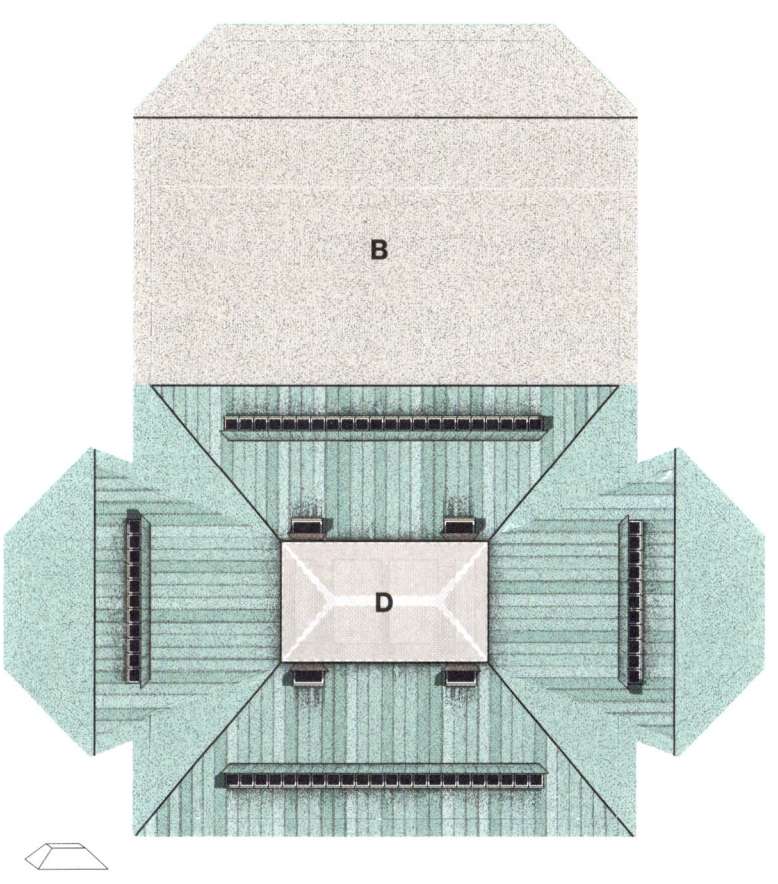
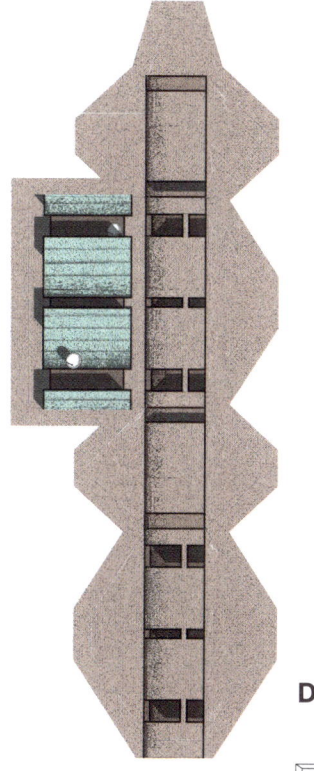

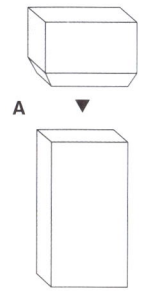 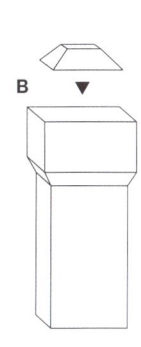 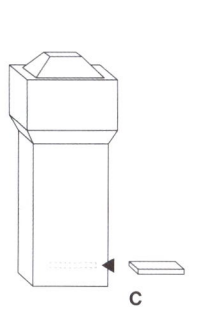 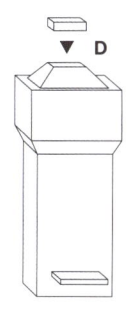 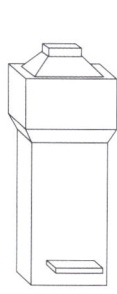

Napoli Vele di Scampia

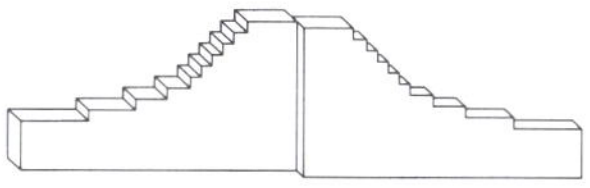

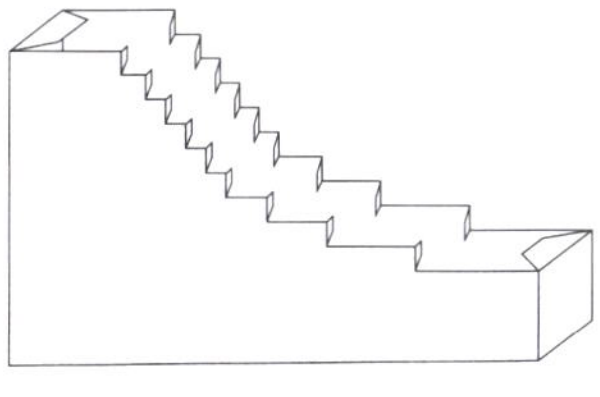

Napoli Vele di Scampia

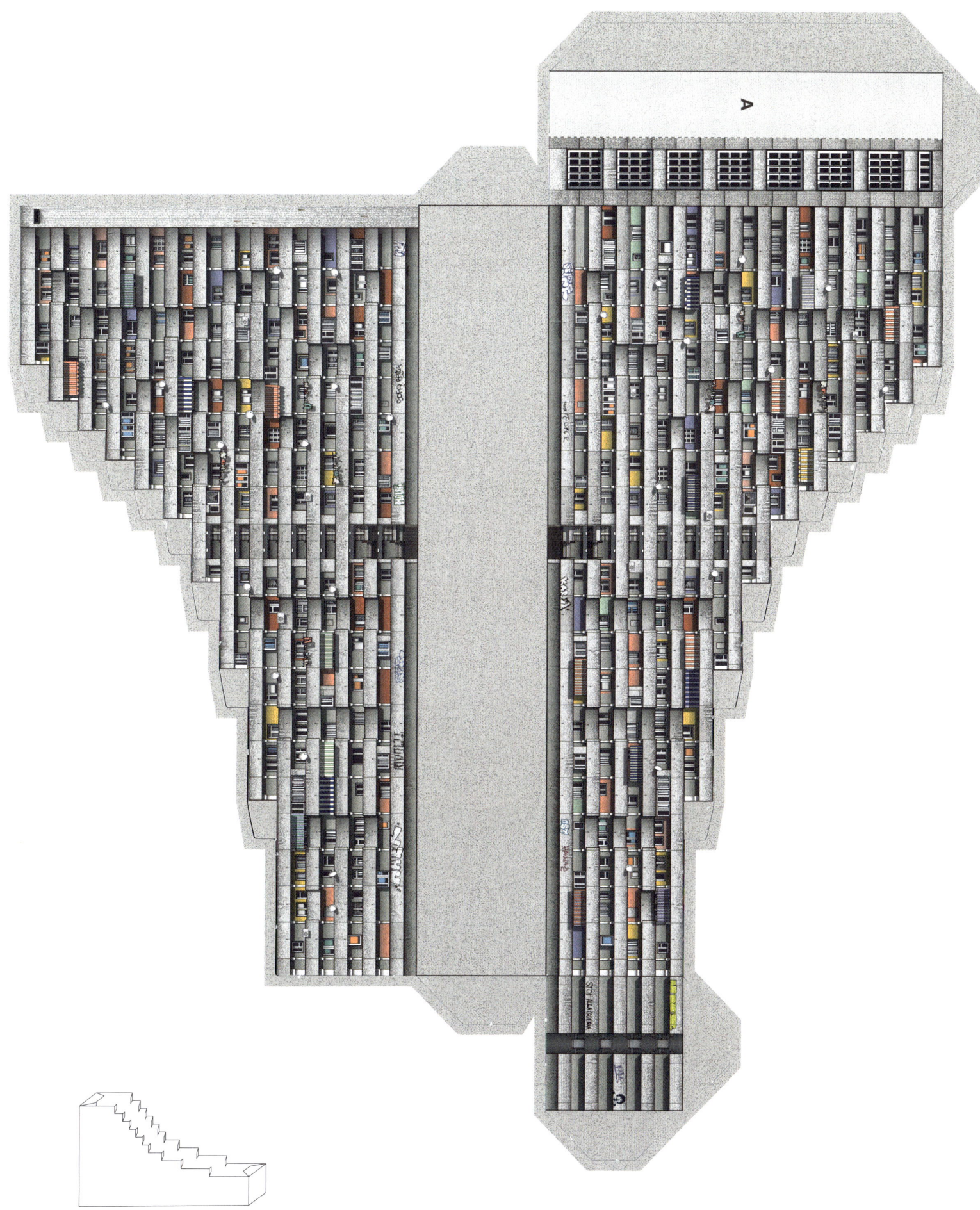

Napoli   Vele di Scampia

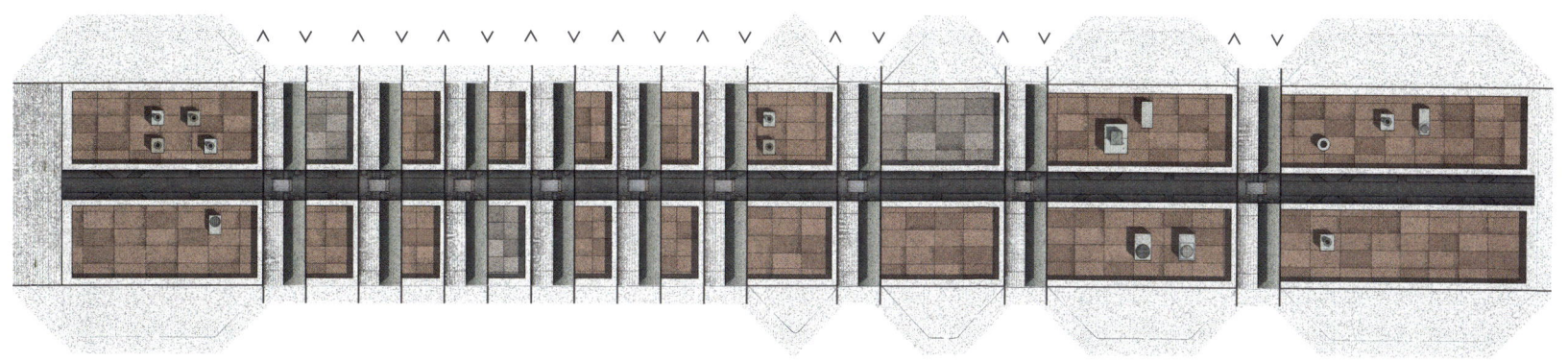

Top   Bottom

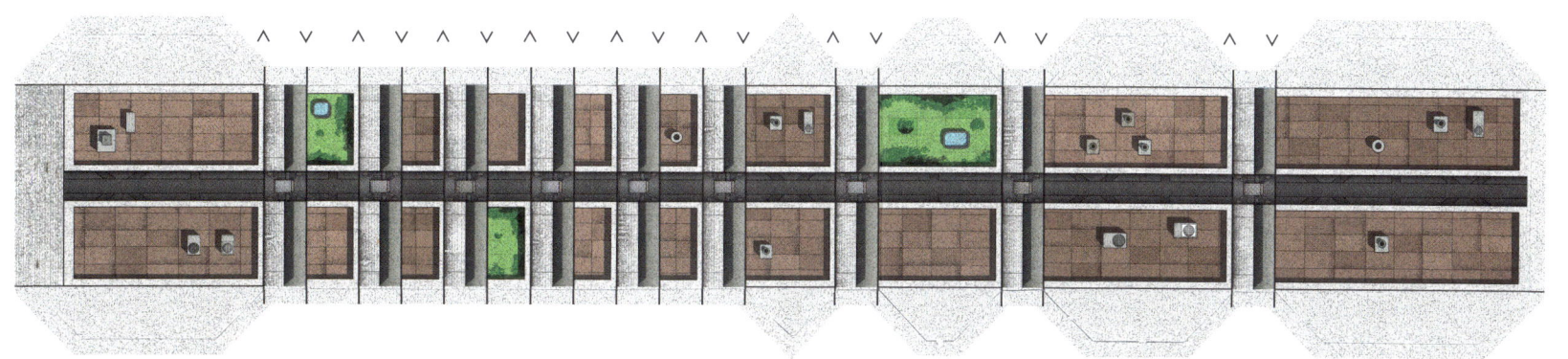

Top   Bottom

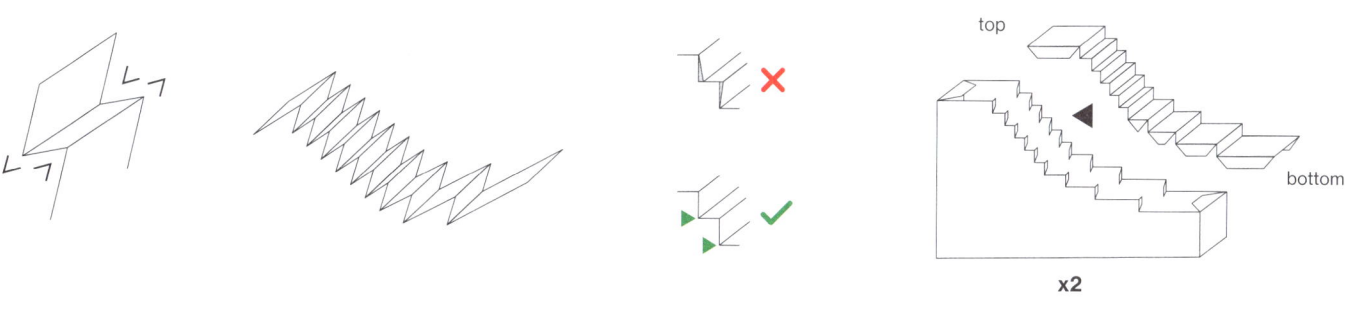

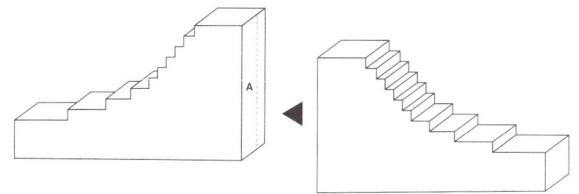

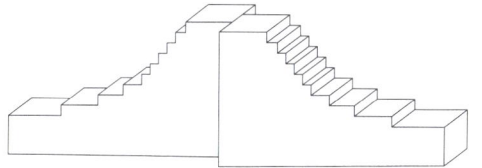

Roma Nuovo Corviale